T0308997

THIS JOURNAL BELONGS TO:

_____

Kindness WILL SAVE the WORLD

A GUIDED JOURNAL

JAMES CREWS

MANDALA

SAN RAFAEL LOS ANGELES LONDON

NO ACT OF KINDNESS IS TOO SMALL

The other day I stopped by a gas station to cash in some scratch-off tickets my husband had bought. We'd won twenty-seven dollars, and I was excited for this windfall of "free money." But when I handed the tickets over to the weary-looking cashier through the slot in the Plexiglas partition, something swept over me. Call it mindfulness, grace, or presence—but I was dropped more deeply into the moment with her on that ordinary morning. For the first time, I noticed her graying hair tied back from her face, and the lines gathered around her mouth, her forehead permanently creased, I thought, from so much worry.

She counted out my winnings in a mechanical way, a heaviness in her husky voice. Before I knew what I was doing, I had lifted a five dollar bill off of the pile of cash and handed it to her. "This was meant for you," I said.

Her whole face changed, shocked by my gesture.

"You don't have to do that," she said, a smile forming on her lips, a hand held to her heart.

I told her I knew that, and said she should treat herself somehow.

As I drove away, I felt the glow of what I had just done, proud of myself for listening to the deeper, truer voice in me, often drowned out by the busyness and noise of daily life. I think we both needed a reminder that kindness does not have to involve grand gestures; it can show up in the smallest of ways and completely shift our days, even the course of our lives.

I am not always compassionate or kind, and often lose the thread of connection I believe is woven through all of us. I hurl angry words at my husband, honk at cars that move too slowly, and sometimes turn away from the pain of others, too afraid of getting involved. But I have learned to celebrate the moments when my own basic goodness takes over, when I see that we are just one species, each doing the best we can with what we have.

During the worst of the pandemic, battling with anxiety and depression, I began keeping a kindness journal as part of my self-care, each morning jotting down the moments, both large and small, when I felt more connected to others. Scanning each day for evidence of tenderness, I trained my mind to find the warmth and light again and again, even in one of my own darkest periods. I also learned to expand my definition of what connection might include. In a given week, kindness was the teller at the bank making eye contact with me through the window of the drive-through, asking about my day. Kindness was the pharmacist at the grocery store taking the time to explain which cortisone cream would best treat the rash on my arm. Kindness was my father-in-law plowing our driveway after a heavy snowstorm, making our house the first stop on his rounds. The entries in my journal later became the essays collected in *Kindness Will Save the World: Stories of Compassion & Connection.*

I invite you to use this journal, adapted from that book, as a way of training yourself to hold on to your own moments of kindness, both past and present. You can write from the quotes and prompts provided, or let them lead you in your own directions. Remember that journaling is your own form of self-care, and there is no right or wrong way to write. The best advice is to write for yourself and just let the words flow. If you ever feel stuck about what to say, try this: Think back to the past few days, and begin, "This week, kindness was . . ." and fill in the blank. For example, I might write: "This week, kindness was my husband making me his famous cornmeal pancakes on a morning when he knew I had to go to work early. Kindness was my Aunt Linda texting me out of the blue to tell me how much she loves me. Kindness was my friend Elizabeth telling me how much she liked the poem I shared with her, and passing it on to her friends."

Give yourself permission to redefine what true connection means to you. Kindness might include the cup of hot chocolate you bought for yourself after lunch, or the few extra minutes you spent chatting with a neighbor because you sensed he was lonely. Whatever brings you that sudden flood of warmth in the chest counts as kindness. I hope you will find, as I have, that the more you look for small kindnesses, the more often they will find you. Writing down your experiences, celebrating the kindness you gave or received, will keep your heart open to the world. By capturing such moments, we learn to listen to those whispers that tell us: no act of kindness is too small to change a person's life, including our own. Taken together, all of our caring gestures toward each other just might save the world.

We easily forget when someone has been kind to us (and tend to remember when someone has wronged or slighted us), so it's good practice to relive an honest connection over and over, to write it down or tell others about it, in order to prolong that feeling of deeper kinship.

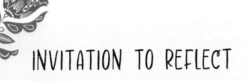

INVITATION TO REFLECT

Describe the last time you felt truly connected to another person, whether it was a friend, family member, or stranger. You might begin with: "I felt an honest connection when _____" and fill in the blank.

KINDNESS IN ACTION

The next time you find yourself remembering a specific moment of kindness, tell someone else about it, and why it has stayed with you. Ask them if they remember any recent times like this, too.

How did it feel to put this kindness into action? Did it turn out the way you had hoped? Why or why not?

_____

_____

_____

_____

_____

_____

_____

_____

_____

_____

_____

_____

_____

_____

_____

_____

_____

_____

_____

_____

RECEIVING KINDNESS

Make a list of recent kindnesses, both large and small, that you have received from others.

SPREADING KINDNESS

Make a list of recent kindnesses, both large and small, that you have spread to others.

_____

_____

_____

_____

_____

_____

_____

_____

_____

_____

_____

_____

_____

_____

_____

_____

_____

_____

_____

_____

_____

_____

_____

_____

If we are positively affected by
someone's kind words or smile,
if we carry that charge for hours after,
then we can remember how easily we
might change someone else's life by
some simple act of care.

INVITATION TO REFLECT

Can you recall a time when some caring gesture changed the course of your life? Maybe it was extra attention or encouragement from a teacher, or when a family member taught you how to do something. How has their kindness stayed with you?

KINDNESS IN ACTION

Make it a practice today to smile at the people you interact with—
the cashiers, baristas, and coworkers all around you. Feel how the
warmth you give others returns to you in surprising ways.

How did it feel to put this kindness into action? Did it turn out the
way you had hoped? Why or why not?

_____

_____

_____

_____

_____

_____

_____

_____

_____

_____

_____

_____

_____

_____

_____

_____

_____

_____

RECEIVING KINDNESS

Make a list of recent kindnesses, both large and small, that you have received from others.

SPREADING KINDNESS

Make a list of recent kindnesses, both large and small, that you have spread to others.

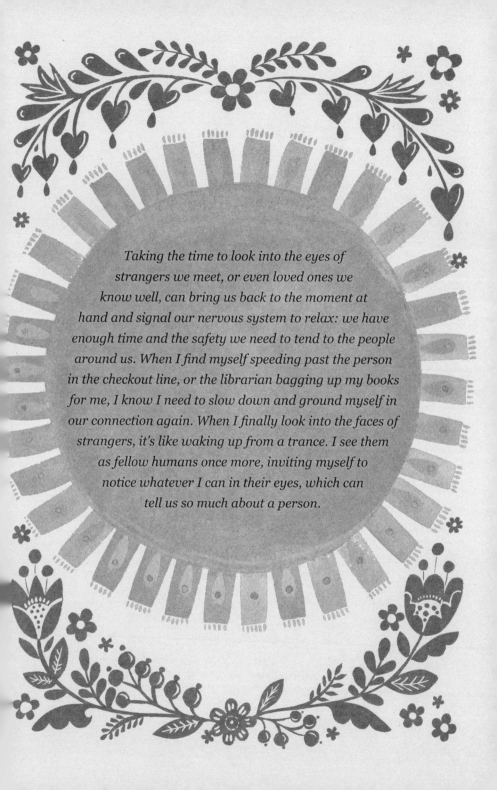

Taking the time to look into the eyes of strangers we meet, or even loved ones we know well, can bring us back to the moment at hand and signal our nervous system to relax: we have enough time and the safety we need to tend to the people around us. When I find myself speeding past the person in the checkout line, or the librarian bagging up my books for me, I know I need to slow down and ground myself in our connection again. When I finally look into the faces of strangers, it's like waking up from a trance. I see them as fellow humans once more, inviting myself to notice whatever I can in their eyes, which can tell us so much about a person.

INVITATION TO REFLECT

We don't always have the time to pause and connect with others, but see if you can remember a recent moment when you let yourself sink into the warmth of connecting with someone else. What did you notice about them, and how did it feel to surrender to kindness?

_____

_____

_____

_____

_____

_____

_____

_____

_____

_____

_____

_____

_____

_____

_____

_____

_____

_____

_____

_____

KINDNESS IN ACTION

The next time you feel yourself in a rush, about to move past some-one without acknowledging them, see if you can slow down and take the risk to connect. Make eye contact and smile. Then feel how your whole day shifts as you create a circle of safety and warmth around you both.

How did it feel to put this kindness into action? Did it turn out the way you had hoped? Why or why not?

_____

_____

_____

_____

_____

_____

_____

_____

_____

_____

_____

_____

_____

_____

_____

_____

RECEIVING KINDNESS

Make a list of recent kindnesses, both large and small, that you have received from others.

SPREADING KINDNESS

Make a list of recent kindnesses, both large and small, that you have spread to others.

When we choose to
share in the joy of another—
and it is often a conscious choice—we
mentally set aside our own concerns
and insecurities. It might take practice
to reach the place of pure joy for a good
friend's new job or someone's marriage,
especially when we wish we had the same.
Yet it can become second nature for us if
we stay aware of our initial reactions
and intentionally link up with the
happiness someone else
is feeling.

INVITATION TO REFLECT

Often, we find ourselves envious of others' good fortune and excitement because we have not been looking after our own joy. Sometimes, life gets so full that we forget what even brings us pleasure in the first place. Make a list of twenty-five small things that bring you joy. You might begin with: "I feel joyful when _____" and fill in the blank, focusing on specific actions and gifts you can offer yourself.

KINDNESS IN ACTION

The next time you feel envious of someone else's accomplishment or good fortune, see if you can generate joy for them anyway. Smile and ask questions, and share how happy you feel for them. We can forget that jealousy and joy for others can coexist at the same time.

How did it feel to put this kindness into action? Did it turn out the way you had hoped? Why or why not?

RECEIVING KINDNESS

Make a list of recent kindnesses, both large and small, that you have received from others.

SPREADING KINDNESS

Make a list of recent kindnesses, both large and small, that you have spread to others.

When I'm locked in worry and anxiety, it's looking outside of myself and noticing the small things that lift me out of the darkness. Seeing red buds on the maple trees or yellow petals bursting forth on the forsythia bush after an endless winter reminds me of rhythms and cycles larger than myself and my own personal suffering.

INVITATION TO REFLECT

What are some of the small things that help lift you out of your own difficult emotions? You might begin with: "When I pause, I notice _____," and fill in the blank, repeating this phrase as you list all the things you see in the world around you.

KINDNESS IN ACTION

The next time you feel anxious and short with the people in your life, take a moment to pause and breathe in. Feel it as an act of kindness to become more mindful and connected to your environment.

How did it feel to put this kindness into action? Did it turn out the way you had hoped? Why or why not?

_____

_____

_____

_____

_____

_____

_____

_____

_____

_____

_____

_____

_____

_____

_____

_____

_____

_____

_____

RECEIVING KINDNESS

Make a list of recent kindnesses, both large and small, that you have received from others.

SPREADING KINDNESS

Make a list of recent kindnesses, both large and small, that you have spread to others.

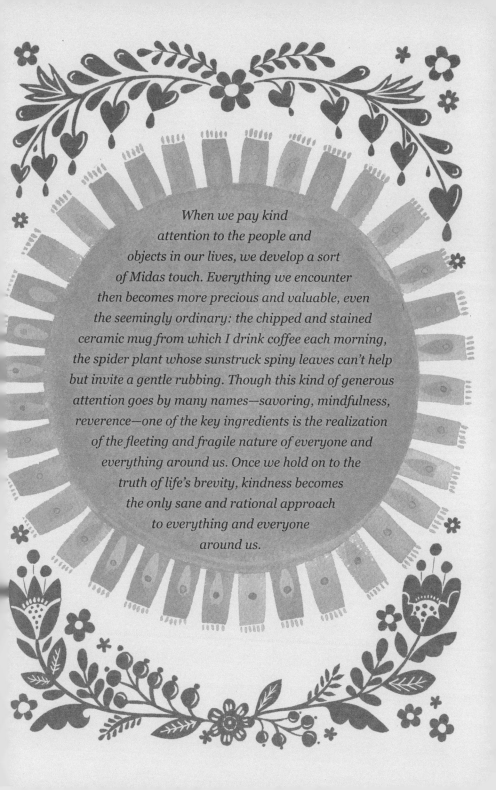

When we pay kind
attention to the people and
objects in our lives, we develop a sort
of Midas touch. Everything we encounter
then becomes more precious and valuable, even
the seemingly ordinary: the chipped and stained
ceramic mug from which I drink coffee each morning,
the spider plant whose sunstruck spiny leaves can't help
but invite a gentle rubbing. Though this kind of generous
attention goes by many names—savoring, mindfulness,
reverence—one of the key ingredients is the realization
of the fleeting and fragile nature of everyone and
everything around us. Once we hold on to the
truth of life's brevity, kindness becomes
the only sane and rational approach
to everything and everyone
around us.

INVITATION TO REFLECT

Take a moment to pause and scan your immediate environment. What are some of the objects around you that may not be "valuable" in the financial sense, but feel precious to you? Make a list of these specific things and the moments with people you love for which you feel especially grateful right now.

KINDNESS IN ACTION

If you enjoyed going out with or talking with a friend, thank them for taking the time. And if someone helped you recently, set aside a few minutes to tell them how much their help meant to you. Offering gratitude to the objects and people in our lives can open the gateway to kindness.

How did it feel to put this kindness into action? Did it turn out the way you had hoped? Why or why not?

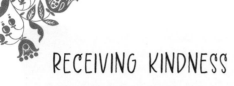

RECEIVING KINDNESS

Make a list of recent kindnesses, both large and small, that you have received from others.

SPREADING KINDNESS

Make a list of recent kindnesses, both large and small, that you have spread to others.

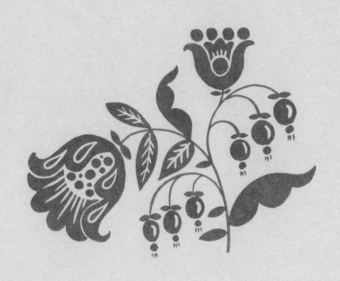

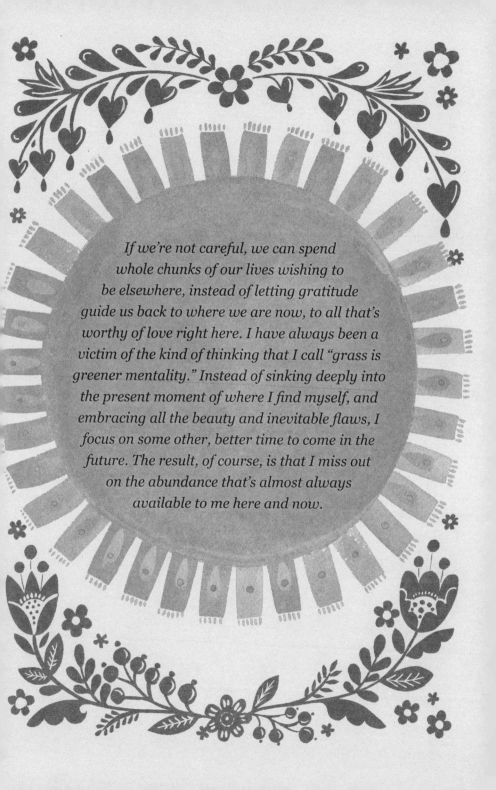

If we're not careful, we can spend whole chunks of our lives wishing to be elsewhere, instead of letting gratitude guide us back to where we are now, to all that's worthy of love right here. I have always been a victim of the kind of thinking that I call "grass is greener mentality." Instead of sinking deeply into the present moment of where I find myself, and embracing all the beauty and inevitable flaws, I focus on some other, better time to come in the future. The result, of course, is that I miss out on the abundance that's almost always available to me here and now.

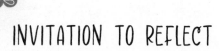

INVITATION TO REFLECT

What gives you a feeling of abundance right now where you are? Make a list of all the ways you've been kind to others recently, all the times you have given something when you didn't have to. No kind and compassionate act is too small to include here.

KINDNESS IN ACTION

The next time you hear that critical inner voice telling you that you don't have enough or that you're not enough, place your hand over your heart and bring to mind all the many ways you've been kind to others over the years, and the ways they've been kind to you. If you feel moved to do so, you might tell someone how their act of kindness has affected you.

How did it feel to put this kindness into action? Did it turn out the way you had hoped? Why or why not?

RECEIVING KINDNESS

Make a list of recent kindnesses, both large and small, that you have received from others.

SPREADING KINDNESS

Make a list of recent kindnesses, both large and small, that you have spread to others.

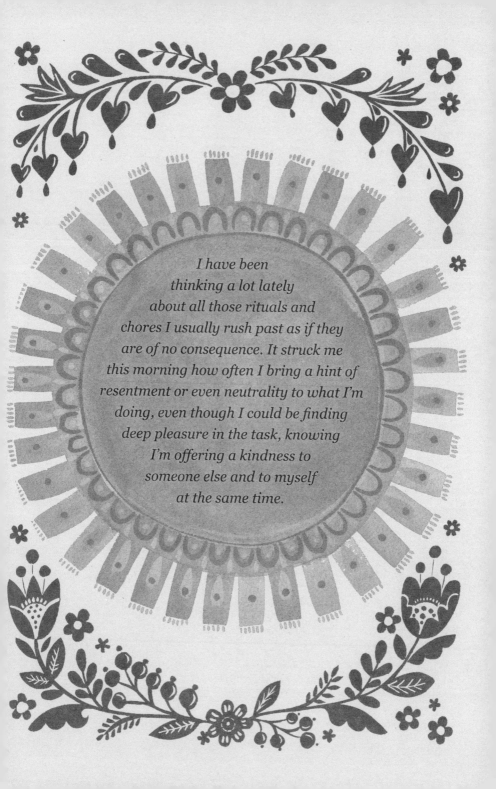

I have been
thinking a lot lately
about all those rituals and
chores I usually rush past as if they
are of no consequence. It struck me
this morning how often I bring a hint of
resentment or even neutrality to what I'm
doing, even though I could be finding
deep pleasure in the task, knowing
I'm offering a kindness to
someone else and to myself
at the same time.

INVITATION TO REFLECT

What are some of the chores that you can't stand to do? Write about a specific moment when you did a favor for someone else and stepped up, even if you didn't want to at first. How did it feel to give so generously?

KINDNESS IN ACTION

Sometimes, we shut down when we sense that people need something from us. The next time this happens, open yourself to the other person and offer to help, even if it feels uncomfortable to do so at first.

How did it feel to put this kindness into action? Did it turn out the way you had hoped? Why or why not?

RECEIVING KINDNESS

Make a list of recent kindnesses, both large and small, that you have received from others.

SPREADING KINDNESS

Make a list of recent kindnesses, both large and small, that you have spread to others.

How often do we turn away from self-love because we believe we don't deserve it, or haven't done enough to earn it? In these anxious times, we can't underestimate the power of self-compassion to turn us into the helpers we'd all rather become, giving what we can to others from a full inner well.

INVITATION TO REFLECT

Describe a period in your life, perhaps even recently, when you ignored your own needs and kept taking care of others. List some of the ways you might bring compassion to yourself during these times, and how you might make other choices to fill up your own inner well. You might begin with: "Self-love is _____," and fill in the blank over and over.

_____

_____

_____

_____

_____

_____

_____

_____

_____

_____

_____

_____

_____

_____

_____

_____

_____

_____

_____

KINDNESS IN ACTION

Make time in the next day or two to offer a specific kindness to yourself, perhaps using an act of self-compassion from your list. Allow yourself to feel grateful for the space and time that will help you heal.

How did it feel to put this kindness into action? Did it turn out the way you had hoped? Why or why not?

RECEIVING KINDNESS

Make a list of recent kindnesses, both large and small, that you have received from others.

SPREADING KINDNESS

Make a list of recent kindnesses, both large and small, that you have spread to others.

It can be easy to fall
into the habit of only giving
to others and brushing aside our
own needs. When we fall out of touch
with ourselves, we need more than a bit of
tenderness to bring ourselves back. We need
radical kindness; the type of deep self-care
that can feel overly indulgent and even
transgressive, but only because we're
used to directing our energy outward,
believing that is the way to
become a better person.

INVITATION TO REFLECT

We end up ignoring our own desires quite often because we believe that self-care is selfish and indulgent. Write about some of the things you'd love to do for yourself but are too afraid of. You might begin with: "If it wasn't so self-indulgent, I would _____" and fill in the blank at least ten times, trying to uncover the small kindnesses you deserve to give to yourself.

KINDNESS IN ACTION

Do something for yourself that feels indulgent, and maybe even silly. Turn off your phone for an hour. Take a walk in a park you've never visited and open all of your senses to nature. Radical kindness often includes forms of rest that we are resisting. Indulge in deep rest this week, creating habits of self-care that renew you and allow you to be even more kind to others in the process.

How did it feel to put this kindness into action? Did it turn out the way you had hoped? Why or why not?

_____

_____

_____

_____

_____

_____

_____

_____

_____

_____

_____

_____

_____

_____

_____

RECEIVING KINDNESS

Make a list of recent kindnesses, both large and small, that you have received from others.

SPREADING KINDNESS

Make a list of recent kindnesses, both large and small, that you have spread to others.

MANDALA

An Imprint of MandalaEarth
PO Box 3088
San Rafael, CA 94912
www.MandalaEarth.com

Find us on Facebook: www.facebook.com/MandalaEarth
Follow us on Twitter: @MandalaEarth

Publisher Raoul Goff
Associate Publisher Roger Shaw
Editorial Director Katie Killebrew
Senior Editor Karyn Gerhard
Editorial Assistant Jon Ellis
VP, Creative Chrissy Kwasnik
Art Director Ashley Quackenbush
Production Designer Amy Tang
VP, Manufacturing Alix Nicholaeff
Production Associate Tiffani Patterson
Sr Production Manager, Subsidiary Rights Lina s Palma-Temena

Text © 2024 James Crews

Illustrations by Dinara Mirtalipova

ISBN: 979-8-88762-006-0

Manufactured in China by Insight Editions
10 9 8 7 6 5 4 3 2 1

ROOTS of PEACE   REPLANTED PAPER

Insight Editions, in association with Roots of Peace, will plant two trees for each tree used in
the manufacturing of this book. Roots of Peace is an internationally renowned humanitarian
organization dedicated to eradicating land mines worldwide and converting war-torn lands into
productive farms and wildlife habitats. Roots of Peace will plant two million fruit and nut trees in
Afghanistan and provide farmers there with the skills and support necessary for sustainable land use.